Roll of Thunder, Hear My Cry
Lit Link

Grades 4-6

Written by Nat Reed

Illustrated by S&S Learning Materials

About the author:
Nat Reed has been a member of the teaching profession for over 30 years. He is presently a full-time instructor at Trent University in the Teacher Education Program.

ISBN: 978-1-55495-033-1
Copyright 2009

All Rights Reserved * Printed in Canada

Published in the U.S.A by:
On The Mark Press
3909 Witmer Road PMB 175
Niagara Falls, New York
14305
www.onthemarkpress.com

Published in Canada by:
S&S Learning Materials
15 Dairy Avenue
Napanee, Ontario
K7R 1M4
www.sslearning.com

Permission to Reproduce

Permission is granted to the individual teacher who purchases one copy of this book to reproduce the student activity material for use in his/her classroom only. Reproduction of these materials for an entire school or for a school system, or for other colleagues or for commercial sale is strictly prohibited. No part of this publication may be transmitted in any form or by any means, electronic, mechanical, recording or otherwise without the prior written permission of the publisher. "We acknowledge the financial support of the Government of Canada through the Book Publishing Industry Development Program (BPIDP) for this project."

At A Glance

Learning Expectations	Chapter 1	Chapter 2	Chapter 3	Chapter 4	Chapter 5	Chapter 6	Chapter 7	Chapter 8	Chapter 9	Chapter 10	Chapter 11	Chapter 12
Reading Comprehension												
• Identify and describe story elements	•	•	•	•	•	•	•	•	•	•	•	•
• Summarize events/details	•	•	•	•	•	•	•	•	•	•	•	•
Reasoning & Critical Thinking Skills												
• Character traits, comparisons	•	•	•	•	•		•		•			
• Use context clues	•	•		•	•	•	•	•		•	•	
• Make inferences (i.e., why events occurred, characters' thoughts and feelings, etc.)	•	•	•	•	•	•	•	•	•	•		•	•
• Determine the meaning of colloquialisms and other phrases		•			•	•		•				
• Understand abstract concepts – conscience, revenge, fear, perseverance, self-respect, exaggeration, conflict, etc.	•	•	•	•	•	•	•	•			•	•
• Develop opinions and personal interpretations	•	•	•	•	•	•	•	•	•	•	•	•
• Write a letter/newspaper editorial						•						
• Conduct an interview								•		•	•	
• Identify/create a *simile*	•				•							
• Identify a *cliffhanger*						•					•	
• Identify *foreshadowing*		•							•			
• Identify an *analogy*											•	
• Identify/create an *alliteration*					•							
• Identify/create *personification*			•		•							
• Identify *conflict*									•		•	
• Identify the *climax* of a story												•
• Develop a collage											•	
• Create a book cover												•
• Create a film review												•
• Create a storyboard												•
• Create an Observation Chart										•		
• Practice research skills	•	•		•								
• Create a synopsis				•	•		•	•	•	•	•	
• Predict an outcome						•		•			•	
Vocabulary Development, Grammar, & Word Usage												
• Identify synonyms, antonyms, and homonyms		•		•	•				•	•	•	•
• Identify syllables			•									
• Identify parts of speech				•						•	•	
• Dictionary and thesaurus skills	•	•	•	•	•	•	•	•	•	•	•	•
• Use words correctly in sentences	•	•	•	•	•	•	•	•	•	•	•	•
• Place words in alphabetical order						•						
• Identify singular/plural				•								
• Identify root words										•		
• Using capitals, correct punctuation							•					

ROLL OF THUNDER, HEAR MY CRY
BY MILDRED D. TAYLOR

Table of Contents

ROLL OF THUNDER, HEAR MY CRY

BY MILDRED D. TAYLOR

Overall Expectations

The students will:

- develop their skills in reading, writing, listening, and oral communication.

- use good literature as a vehicle for developing skills required by curriculum expectations: reasoning and critical thinking, knowledge of language structure, vocabulary building, and use of conventions.

- become meaningfully engaged in the drama of literature through a variety of types of questions and activities.

- identify and describe elements of stories (i.e., plot, main idea, characters, setting).

- learn and review many skills in order to develop good reading habits.

- provide clear answers to questions and well-constructed explanations.

- organize and classify information to clarify thinking.

- learn about the dynamics of unselfish relationships, the destructive power of greed, prejudice and hatred, and the ability to exercise initiative in difficult circumstances.

- appreciate the importance of self discipline and loyalty in friendship

- relate events and feelings of characters found in the novel to their own lives and experiences.

- appreciate the importance of loyalty in friendship, family, in personal relationships, and the risks involved in cultivating friendships.

- learn about the necessity of maintaining hope in the face of unfortunate circumstances.

- appreciate that the growth of one's character is often the result of trials that come into one's life.

- learn the importance of dealing with adversity and developing perseverance in the face of difficult experiences.

- state their own interpretation of a written work, using evidence from the novel and from their own knowledge and experience.

ROLL OF THUNDER, HEAR MY CRY

BY MILDRED D. TAYLOR

List of Skills

Vocabulary Development

1. Using content clues
2. Locating descriptive words/phrases
3. Listing synonyms, antonyms, homonyms
4. Use of capitals and punctuation
5. Identifying syllables
6. Understanding *colloquialisms*
7. Determining alphabetical order
8. Use of singular/plural nouns
9. Developing dictionary skills
10. Identifying parts of speech
11. Identify an *analogy*
12. Identifying *personification*
13. Identifying a *simile*
14. Identifying *alliteration*

Setting Activities

1. Identify the details of a setting
2. Investigating The Great Depression
3. Investigating Jefferson Davis County, Mississippi

Plot Activities

1. Identify *conflict* in the story
2. Determine the role of others in one's personal growth
3. Develop a Storyboard
4. Identify a *cliffhanger*
5. Identify the climax of a novel
6. Create a synopsis

Character Activities

1. Determine character traits
2. Compare two characters
3. Relating personal experiences
4. Understand concepts: *self-respect, perseverance*

Creative and Critical Thinking

1. Research
2. Complete Observation Chart
3. Write a letter
4. Conduct an interview
5. Create a film review
6. Write a description of personal feelings

Art Activities

1. Design a collage
2. Design a cover for the novel
3. Develop a Storyboard

ROLL OF THUNDER, HEAR MY CRY
BY MILDRED D. TAYLOR

Teacher Suggestions

This resource can be used in a variety of ways:

1. The student booklet focuses on one chapter of the novel at a time. Each of these sections contains the following activities:
   a. **Before you read the chapters** (reasoning and critical thinking skills)
   b. **Vocabulary building** (dictionary and thesaurus skills)
   c. **Questions on the chapter** (reading comprehension skills)
   d. **Language activities** (grammar, punctuation, word structure, and extension activities)

2. Students may read the novel at their own speed and then select, or be assigned, a variety of questions and activities.

3. **Bulletin Board and Interest Center Ideas:** Themes might include: The Great Depression (1930's); Mississippi; cotton (agriculture of the southern U.S.); automobiles of the 1930's (i.e., Packard).

4. **Pre-Reading Activities.** Roll of Thunder, Hear My Cry may also be used in conjunction with themes of racial prejudice; bullying; self-esteem; the importance of family; friendship; facing adversity; developing personal responsibility.

5. **Independent Reading Approach:** Students who are able to work independently may attempt to complete the assignments in a self-directed manner. Initially these students should participate in the pre-reading activities with the rest of the class. Students should familiarize themselves with the reproducible student booklet. Completed worksheets should be submitted so that the teacher can note how quickly and accurately the students are working. Students may be brought together periodically to discuss issues in specific sections of the novel.

6. **Fine Art Activities:** Students may integrate such topics as art activities using cotton as a resource; a study of artists of the 1920's and 30's; themes from the Great Depression (i.e., technology, public figures, etc.); collages; a Storyboard; book covers.

7. Encourage the students to keep a reading log in which they record their readings each day and their thoughts about the passage.

8. Students should keep all their work together in one place. A portfolio cover is provided for this reason.

9. Students should not be expected to complete all activities. Teachers should allow choice and in some cases match the activity to the student's ability.

10. Students should keep track (in their portfolio) of the activities they complete.

ROLL OF THUNDER, HEAR MY CRY
BY MILDRED D. TAYLOR

Synopsis

Roll of Thunder, Hear My Cry is Mildred D. Taylor's renowned novel set in Mississippi during the Great Depression. It tells the story of the Logans, an independent, hard-working African-American family who are locked in a desperate struggle to survive during desperate times, and hang on to the 400 acres of land that Grandpa Logan has passed down to them. Told through the eyes of ten-year old Cassie, the novel graphically portrays a South of segregation, lynch mobs, and the social and economic hardships endured by the black people of the region.

Taylor has said that she hopes that this novel *"will one day be instrumental in teaching children of all colors the tremendous influence Cassie's generation had in bringing about the Civil Rights movement of the fifties and sixties."*

Perhaps the most memorable feature of the novel is the portrayal of the Logan family: a close-knit group of people with a common purpose – maintaining their hold on the land, which gives them a solid place in this world.

Author Biography
Mildred D. Taylor

Mildred D. Taylor was born in Jackson, Mississippi in 1943, the same state as the setting of *Roll of Thunder, Hear My Cry*. Raised in Toledo, Ohio, Mildred loved to listen to the stories told by her father and other family members about her grandparents and other ancestors. As she heard more and more of these stories, she realized how different they were from the stories she read in textbooks. In high school, she already knew that she wanted to be a writer. After graduating from the University of Toledo, she joined the Peace Corps and served in Ethiopia teaching English to Ethiopian children. After obtaining her Masters Degree in Journalism, she moved to Los Angeles, where she worked during the day and wrote at night.

Mildred's first book was a novella, **Song of the Trees**, and featured the same cast of characters as *Roll of Thunder, Hear My Cry*. Cassie Logan is a composite of several people, including a beloved aunt of the author. The love of the land is a repeated theme throughout Mildred's novels. Mildred is the author of three realistic novels which highlight the security of family love against the evils of racism, *Roll of Thunder, Hear My Cry, Song of the Trees*, and *Let the Circle Be Unbroken*.

ROLL OF THUNDER, HEAR MY CRY
BY MILDRED D. TAYLOR

Student Checklist

Student Name: _____ Date: _____

Assignment	Grade/Level	Comments

ROLL OF THUNDER, HEAR MY CRY

BY MILDRED D. TAYLOR

Name: _____

ROLL OF THUNDER, HEAR MY CRY
BY MILDRED D. TAYLOR

Chapter 1

Before you read the chapter:

Martin Luther King Jr. once said, *Injustice anywhere is a threat to justice everywhere.*
In Chapter One, the reader is confronted with many forms of injustice. Do you think if everyone followed the golden rule *(treat others as you want to be treated),* injustice would be eliminated in the world? Defend your answer.

_____

_____

_____

_____

Vocabulary:

Choose a word from the list to complete each sentence.

imperious	restrain	disdain	concession	meticulous	indignation
amiable	dubious	vigorous	morose	torment	admonish

1. When it came to his penmanship, Scott was very _____.

2. Shirley was a little _____ about whether Terri was actually telling the truth.

3. It is doubtful that the government will make a meaningful _____ in the court case.

4. Principal Perkins began to _____ the children about their inappropriate behavior.

5. "Please try your best to _____ yourselves when the prince visits," she advised.

6. Despite her lack of sleep, Aunt Sara was in an _____ mood.

7. His _____ of all things Western was most evident.

ROLL OF THUNDER, HEAR MY CRY

BY MILDRED D. TAYLOR

8. Since his parents' accident, Peter has become more and more _____.

9. The mosquitoes made my holiday in the north country a living _____.

10. Historians say that Queen Victoria was a most _____ monarch.

11. There is nothing like fifteen minutes of _____ exercise to wake one up in the morning.

12. When his aide hinted that he was a liar, the President was filled with _____.

Questions:

1. Why did Papa have to find work?

    _____

    _____

2. From what we know about Grandpa, what proof do we have that he was a good leader of the Logan family?

    _____

    _____

3. Describe the dirty trick that T.J. played on Claude.

    _____

    _____

4. How did Little Man get dirty?

    _____

    _____

5. Why did Miss Crocker have to teach two classes that morning?

    _____

    _____

ROLL OF THUNDER, HEAR MY CRY
BY MILDRED D. TAYLOR

6. a) What caused Little Man to object to the book he had been given?

_____

_____

b) Do you feel Little Man was justified in the way he reacted? Explain your answer.

_____

_____

7. Why do you think that the teacher, Miss Crocker, chooses to overlook the insulting word that has upset Little Man?

_____

_____

8. Give your impression of how Mama handled the confrontation with Miss Crocker. Do you think she handled it wisely, or should she have done something different? Defend your answer.

_____

_____

_____

9. Character Match

Match each member of the Logan family from Chapter One with the correct description:

1. Little Man   a) a short, round boy of seven

2. Stacey   b) youngest brother; values cleanliness

3. Christopher-John   c) a teacher at Great Faith Elementary and Secondary School

4. Cassie   d) 12 years old, in a grouchy mood

5. Big Ma   e) in the fourth grade

6. Mama   f) the children's grandmother

ROLL OF THUNDER, HEAR MY CRY
BY MILDRED D. TAYLOR

Language Activity:

Simile

a) A *simile* is used to compare two things, usually with the words "like" or "as." An example from this chapter is: *Before us the narrow, sun-splotched road wound like a lazy red serpent...* In this simile what two things are being compared?

_____

_____

b) Create your own simile using an object from your classroom as the subject.

_____

_____

Extension Activity:

Investigate **one** of the following three topics from Chapter One, researching three interesting facts about your choice.

The Great Depression	
Jefferson Davis County, Mississippi	
Jefferson Davis	

ROLL OF THUNDER, HEAR MY CRY

BY MILDRED D. TAYLOR

Chapter 2

Before you read the chapter:

Someone said that "Roll of Thunder, Hear My Cry" is *a tale full of painful life lessons*. How do you think that this statement might prove to be true from what you have read so far?

_____

_____

_____

Vocabulary:

Using words from this chapter, complete the following crossword puzzle.

DEACONS	FLIRTING	STRAWBERRY	GREAT	POUR	GAIT	ANY
SASS	SPIN	SMELLINGS	DATES	STILL	HOT	TO
WAIST	THUNDER	ENCOUNTER	LOGAN	ED	SORT	AGES
SORRY	BERRY	BOOTLEG	MINT	AVERY	FLEES	DEFIED
MISSISSIPPI	STACEY	HENRY	DELICATE	COTTON	ATTEMPT	BODY

ROLL OF THUNDER, HEAR MY CRY

BY MILDRED D. TAYLOR

DOWN

1. Playing at love.
2. Particular days, months, and years.
3. Runs away.
4. Fragile; easily broken or damaged.
6. Large in number.
7. A corpse.
8. Last name of man who was killed by the mob.
9. John _____ Berry.
13. Church officials.
14. Quiet; unmoving.
16. Try.
18. A family that visited the Logans in this chapter.
19. The length of time people live.
21. Cassie's brother.
23. An herb or a tasty candy.
24. To arrange according to kind (i.e., socks).
25. To turn rapidly.
26. Please _____ me a glass of milk.
27. Not cold.

ACROSS

2. Challenged or resisted.
5. Cassie's surname.
8. To deal in liquor or other goods unlawfully.
10. Short for Edward.
11. A small red fruit.
12. To talk back disrespectfully.
14. Regret.
15. The part of the human body between the ribs and the hips.
17. Manner of walking or running.
20. A crop grown in Mississippi.
21. _____ Creek.
22. Do you feel _____ better?
23. Cassie's home state.
28. Opposite of from.
29. Meet.
30. Roll of _____ , Hear My Cry.

Questions:

1. a) What was unusual about the appearance of Mr. L.T. Morrison?

    _____

    _____

    b) What reason did Papa give for bringing Mr. Morrison home with him?

    _____

    _____

ROLL OF THUNDER, HEAR MY CRY

BY MILDRED D. TAYLOR

c) What did the children suspect was the <u>real</u> reason Papa brought him home?

_____

_____

2. Mr. Morrison mentions getting fired for fighting. Why was he the only one to get fired?

_____

_____

3. Why did Papa forbid the children from going to the Wallace store?

_____

_____

4. The men who attacked John Henry Berry and the others were obviously very bad people. Consider the kind of people who would do such things and list three characteristics you believe they would possess.

_____

_____

_____

5. What did Papa mean when he said to the children, "I'm gonna wear y'all out?"

_____

_____

ROLL OF THUNDER, HEAR MY CRY
BY MILDRED D. TAYLOR

Language Activities:

The people of Jefferson County, Mississippi, have their own unique way of speaking English. Regional dialects of this kind are often called **colloquialisms**. An example is: *When Henrietta went to the sheriff and told him what she'd seed…* Find two more example of colloquialisms in the novel thus far.

_____

_____

_____

Foreshadowing is a literary device in which an author drops subtle hints about what will happen later in the story. The author compares Mr. Morrison's voice to *the roll of low thunder*. Considering **a)** the title of the novel and **b)** the answer to Question **1c)** above, could this statement be an example of foreshadowing? Explain the reasons for your answer.

_____

_____

_____

_____

_____

Extension Activity:

Cotton was an important crop to many Mississippi families, including the Logans. Investigate cotton and find out the answers:

a) What does the **ginning** process remove? _____

b) In the 19th and early 20 centuries, cotton was known as " _____ Cotton"
of the southern United States because of its economic importance.

c) The seed cases are also known as cotton _____.

d) The cotton fiber is spun into a yarn or _____.

ROLL OF THUNDER, HEAR MY CRY
BY MILDRED D. TAYLOR

Chapter 3

Before you read the chapter:

The driver of the school bus takes great delight in splashing the children walking to school, and his passengers share in his pleasure. There is little doubt that these actions are the work of **bullies**. How is this fact true for not only the bus driver, but his passengers as well?

_____

_____

_____

Benjamin Disraeli, who served as Prime Minister of Great Britain on two occasions, once said, "Courage is fire, but bullying is smoke." What do you think Disraeli meant by this?

_____

_____

_____

Vocabulary:

In each of the following sets of words, underline the one word that does not belong. Then write a sentence explaining why it does not fit.

1. inaccessible   unapproachable   unmovable   unreachable

_____

2. resentful   dejected   sad   melancholy

_____

3. embittered   lonely   irate   furious

_____

ROLL OF THUNDER, HEAR MY CRY
BY MILDRED D. TAYLOR

4.	relent	yield	comply	realize

5.	command	oblivious	heedless	unmindful

6.	intense	vehement	earnest	reckless

7.	defiant	delicious	antagonistic	rebellious

8.	resolve	determine	approve	unravel

9.	contagious	catching	spreading	laughable

10.	startle	tolerate	accept	allow

ROLL OF THUNDER, HEAR MY CRY

BY MILDRED D. TAYLOR

Questions:

Cloze Call

Complete the following exercise filling in the correct words from the **Word Box**.

shotgun	Jason	Grimes	Avery	Stacey	churches
Mama	calfskins	October	bus	Morrison	tool
burn	water	lunch	headlights	limbs	

By the end of _____, the rain began to fall heavily. To shield the children against

the rain, Mama gave them dried _____. To keep dry, however, the children preferred

the shelter of the overhanging _____ in the forest. Mama explained to Little Man that

money which supported the black schools came from the black _____. After being

splashed by the passing bus one particular day, _____ promised Little Man that it

wouldn't happen again, at least not for a long while. At _____ hour, the children took

some shovels from the _____ shed and dug a hole in the middle of the road. The hole

quickly filled with _____. That evening on the way home, the children watched as the

_____ got stuck in the hole. Mr. _____, the driver, was extremely upset.

At home that evening, the children were surprised when _____ said she was glad

the bus had gotten stuck. Later that evening, Joe _____ came by to warn them that

the night men were riding. Little Man was afraid that the night men were going to come and

_____ them up. Later, when Cassie went outside, she was frightened by _____ ,

their hound dog. Just when she was about to go back to bed, a caravan of _____

appeared in the east, coming toward her. After the cars left, Cassie could see Mr. _____

standing in the darkness, a _____ in his hand.

ROLL OF THUNDER, HEAR MY CRY

BY MILDRED D. TAYLOR

Language Activities:

1. Choose <u>ten</u> words from these chapters with two or more **syllables**. Indicate the syllables by drawing a line between each syllable. Example: **some/thing**.

_____   _____

_____   _____

_____   _____

_____   _____

_____   _____

2. A **literary device** the author enjoys using is **personification**. Personification is when an inanimate object (non-living object such as a ship) is given human characteristics.

   An example of this is in the first paragraph when the author writes,

   "At first the rain had merely splotched the dust, which seemed to be rejoicing in its own resiliency and laughing at the heavy drops thudding against it..."

   • What object is personified in this sentence, and what human action(s) is it accomplishing?

   • Think of an interesting inanimate object and create a sentence in which this object is personified.

_____

_____

_____

_____

_____

_____

ROLL OF THUNDER, HEAR MY CRY
BY MILDRED D. TAYLOR

Chapter 4

Before you read the chapter:

In Chapter Four several of the characters prove to be very **honorable** people – even in the face of adversity. In your opinion, what does it mean to be honorable? Tell about a time when you witnessed someone who acted honorably.

_____

_____

_____

_____

Vocabulary:

Draw a straight line to connect the vocabulary word to its definition. Remember to use a straight edge (like a ruler).

1. confirm	a) to explain
2. intend	b) careful
3. expound	c) revealed
4. feign	d) forceful
5. discreet	e) support
6. engrossed	f) titleholder; manager
7. disclosed	g) blend; mix
8. emphatic	h) to have in mind
9. disrupt	i) lost in; rapt
10. intermingle	j) pretend
11. patronize	k) validate
12. proprietor	l) disturb

ROLL OF THUNDER, HEAR MY CRY
BY MILDRED D. TAYLOR

Questions:

1. As this chapter opens, Cassie is busy **churning**. **Investigate** and describe what is involved in this process.

   _____

   _____

2. Big Ma and Mama are concerned about Cassie at the beginning of this chapter. What <u>three</u> symptoms concerned Big Ma?

   _____

   _____

3. What strategy did the Logan children use in order to get T.J. to tell stories that interested them?

   _____

   _____

4. Why did the night riders pay a visit to Mr. Tatum and what did they do to him?

   _____

   _____

5. Why did Mr. Morrison prefer to stay in the old shack, even though he was invited to stay in the house?

   _____

   _____

6. Why did Stacey resent Mr. Morrison?

   _____

   _____

ROLL OF THUNDER, HEAR MY CRY
BY MILDRED D. TAYLOR

7. a) Write a brief synopsis describing how Stacey got into trouble at school and what he decided to do about it.

_____

_____

_____

_____

_____

   b) What dilemma did Stacey encounter regarding the Wallace store?

_____

_____

8. What decision did Mr. Morrison make regarding the incident at the Wallace store? What does this tell you about his character?

_____

_____

_____

9. Why did Mr. Granger want to buy the Logans' land?

_____

_____

10. Describe what happened to Mr. Berry.

_____

_____

11. What steps does Mama take to discourage others from doing business with the Wallaces?

_____

_____

ROLL OF THUNDER, HEAR MY CRY
BY MILDRED D. TAYLOR

Language Activities:

Write the plural of the following nouns from this chapter. Careful – you may wish to consult a dictionary for some of these words.

Singular Noun	Plural Noun
1. child	
2. man	
3. bus	
4. buddy	
5. class	
6. gully	
7. folk	
8. family	
9. match	
10. berry	

Alliteration

Alliteration is the repetition of the first consonant sound in a phrase.

An example is: *She sells seashells by the seashore.* An example from Chapter Four: *lifted a still-swinging Stacey off T.J.*

Create your own alliterations using the following ideas:

a) Describe a glass shattering on the floor.

b) Describe the sound of a rainstorm.

_____

c) Invent your own idea here!

_____

Extension Activity:

The night riders of this novel were probably members of an organization known as the **Ku Klux Klan**. Investigate this organization and write a brief report outlining its origins, purpose, and history.

_____

_____

_____

_____

_____

_____

_____

Character Study

Chapter Four provides many opportunities to get to know the true characters of many of the people in this novel. For each person below, write one word which you think best describes his or her personality/character.

Mr. Morrison	
Big Ma	
Stacey	
Mama	
T.J.	

ROLL OF THUNDER, HEAR MY CRY
BY MILDRED D. TAYLOR

Chapter 5

Before you read the chapter:

Chapter Five concludes with the statement, "No day in all my life had ever been as cruel as this one." Predict what you think might happen to Cassie to make her have such a terrible day.

_____

_____

_____

_____

Vocabulary:

Choose a word from the list that means the same (synonym) or nearly the same as the word in bold print.

| disgust | reluctant | warily | retaliate | obvious | persisted |
| denied | envision | ambled | prevail | moderate | obnoxious |

1. Did you think you would **surmount** all obstacles?	
2. He **disavowed** knowing anyone in my family.	
3. It was **plain** that he was telling the truth.	
4. T.J. was a most **annoying** boy.	
5. Did anyone ever **dream** that he would one day be Prime Minister?	
6. She **strolled** casually up to the store.	
7. The two children walked across the ice very **carefully**.	
8. The prince was very **hesitant** about taking over as king.	
9. He **endured** through many forms of persecution.	
10. The temperatures in Toronto are quite **reasonable**.	
11. When the police officer saw the crime being committed, he was filled with **repulsion**.	
12. It is usually not a good idea to **get even** when someone offends you.	

ROLL OF THUNDER, HEAR MY CRY
BY MILDRED D. TAYLOR

Questions:

1. What was Big Ma's motivation in bringing the children along with her to Strawberry?

   _____

   _____

2. What time did they leave for town?

   _____

   _____

3. What was Cassie's initial reaction to seeing the town of Strawberry for the first time?

   _____

   _____

4. Why couldn't the Logans sell their produce nearer the entrance?

   _____

   _____

5. Write a brief synopsis of the incident between Cassie and Mr. Barnett.

   _____

   _____

6. Choose one appropriate adjective to describe the personalities of the following people:

   T.J. _____   Jeremy _____

   Mr. Simms _____   Lillian Jean _____

ROLL OF THUNDER, HEAR MY CRY

BY MILDRED D. TAYLOR

Language Activities:

Place the following words from this chapter in **alphabetical order.**

Strawberry	1.	_____
subdued	2.	_____
surprisingly	3.	_____
suppose	4.	_____
Stacey	5.	_____
such	6.	_____
sense	7.	_____
several	8.	_____
shingles	9.	_____
suggestion	10.	_____

Express Yourself:

a) Put each of these expressions from Chapter Five in your own words (you may have to check the context of the expressions):

while the world lay black _____

_____

A gutting disappointment enveloping me _____

_____

People from the store began to ring the Simmes _____

_____

b) Identify the literary devices from this chapter:

he was fully awake and chattering like a cockatoo _____

a paved road which cut through its center and fled northward _____

ROLL OF THUNDER, HEAR MY CRY
BY MILDRED D. TAYLOR

Before you read the chapter:

Without consulting any references, write a brief definition for the word prejudice below and give an example.

_____

_____

_____

_____

Vocabulary:

Solve the following word search puzzle using the words from the **Word Box**. Remember – the words can be horizontal, vertical or diagonal. They may be forward or even backward!

AUDIBLE	ALOOF	REPRIMAND	OMINOUS	CONFIDENT
RETALIATE	RESPECT	CHIGNON	FRUSTRATE	SECRETIVE
LUXURY	HESITATE	RESIST	PROTEST	INTERSECT

L	U	X	U	R	Y	Q	W	E	R	T	Y	U	I	A
I	A	A	S	D	N	A	M	I	R	P	E	R	L	Q
H	N	U	S	C	D	F	G	H	J	K	L	O	Z	X
E	X	T	D	C	H	V	B	N	M	Q	O	W	E	R
S	P	O	E	I	I	I	U	Y	T	F	R	E	W	Q
I	L	K	J	R	B	H	G	T	G	F	D	S	A	T
T	S	M	N	B	S	L	C	N	V	C	X	Z	A	S
A	U	F	G	H	J	E	E	K	O	L	Z	X	C	E
T	O	H	G	F	P	D	C	S	A	N	Z	X	C	T
E	N	F	G	S	E	V	I	T	E	R	C	E	S	O
P	I	O	E	I	U	E	T	A	I	L	A	T	E	R
U	M	R	F	R	U	S	T	R	A	T	E	U	Y	P
C	O	N	F	I	D	E	N	T	T	S	I	S	E	R

ROLL OF THUNDER, HEAR MY CRY

BY MILDRED D. TAYLOR

Questions:

1. Why didn't Big Ma take Cassie's side in her dispute with Mr. Simms?

   _____

   _____

2. Why didn't Big Ma want Cassie to tell Uncle Hammer what happened in town? How might Big Ma have averted this problem?

   _____

   _____

3. Explain what Mama meant by the statement: *"that's the way of things, Cassie?"*

   _____

   _____

4. Give your impression of Mama's explanation of Mr. Simms' behaviour toward Cassie: *"Because he's one of those people who has to believe that white people are better than black people to make himself feel big."* Is Mama correct? Is there any other explanation for the way Mr. Simms behaved?

   _____

   _____

5. Why didn't Papa Luke's owners try to break him?

   _____

   _____

6. Mama says to Cassie, "I think you've done enough growing up for one day, Cassie." How had Cassie *grown up* on this particular day?

   _____

   _____

ROLL OF THUNDER, HEAR MY CRY
BY MILDRED D. TAYLOR

7. How had Mr. Morrison prevented Uncle Hammer from getting revenge on Mr. Simms?

_____

_____

8. Explain why T.J. reacted the way he did to Stacey's new coat.

_____

_____

Language Activities:

Rewrite the following sentences putting in the **correct capitalization** and **punctuation**.

1. cassie and stacey drove into strawberry in uncle hammer's packard

_____

_____

2. why don't you go to boston for the christmas holiday

_____

_____

3. france germany and belgium are all european countries

_____

_____

Cliffhanger

A **cliffhanger** is a literary device in which a chapter contains an abrupt ending, often leaving the main characters in a precarious or difficult situation. How might it be said that Chapter Six ends with a cliffhanger? Why do you suppose an author uses this device?

_____

_____

ROLL OF THUNDER, HEAR MY CRY
BY MILDRED D. TAYLOR

Extension Activity:

The last couple of days have certainly proved most traumatic for Cassie – her trip to Strawberry, and then Uncle Hammer's visit. Imagine you are Cassie and write a brief letter to your dad describing the events of the last couple of days and your feelings. (Be careful to describe the events in such a way that they don't upset your dad too much!)

ROLL OF THUNDER, HEAR MY CRY
BY MILDRED D. TAYLOR

Chapter 7

Before you read the chapter:

When do you think it is worth making a personal sacrifice to stand up for something important that you believe in? Can you think of an example from your own experiences when this happened (or might happen in the future) – or an example you heard or read about?

_____

_____

_____

_____

_____

Vocabulary:

Write a **sentence** using the following words. Make sure that the meaning of the word is clear in your sentence.

inaudible: _____

_____

apprehensive: _____

_____

console: _____

_____

ROLL OF THUNDER, HEAR MY CRY
BY MILDRED D. TAYLOR

interminable: _____

_____

adored: _____

_____

escorting: _____

_____

resemblance: _____

_____

malevolent: _____

_____

affirmed: _____

_____

boycott: _____

_____

Questions:

1. a) When Uncle Hammer discovered that Stacey had given his coat to T.J., what was Uncle Hammer's message to Stacey in a nutshell?

_____

_____

_____

ROLL OF THUNDER, HEAR MY CRY
BY MILDRED D. TAYLOR

1. b) How did Stacey react to Uncle Hammer's message to him?

   _____

   _____

2. Why did Cassie know it was safe to talk to Papa about the incident with the Simms in Strawberry?

   _____

   _____

3. What did it mean for slaves to be of **breeded stock**?

   _____

   _____

4. Why did Stacey and Cassie receive books written by **Alexander Dumas** for Christmas?

   _____

   _____

5. Why do you think the Avery family was invited to the Logans' Christmas dinner?

   _____

   _____

6. Why do you think Jeremy paid the Logans a visit on Christmas and gave Stacey the gift?

   _____

   _____

7. Why do you think Stacey put the flute in his box of treasured things and never played with it again?

   _____

   _____

ROLL OF THUNDER, HEAR MY CRY
BY MILDRED D. TAYLOR

8. Why did Big Ma transfer the title of the land over to her children?

_____

_____

9. What generous thing did Mr. Jamison volunteer to do?

_____

_____

10. Describe how Mr. Granger attempted to intimidate the Logans.

_____

_____

_____

11. What is the worst thing that can happen to the Logan family? Predict what you think will come of Mr. Granger's threats.

_____

_____

_____

_____

ROLL OF THUNDER, HEAR MY CRY

BY MILDRED D. TAYLOR

Extension Activities:

Choose any <u>two</u> characters you've already met in this novel. **Compare** four things about these two people. Consider such things as physical appearance, personality, age, talents, attitude, etc.

Character 1 Name: _____	Character 2 Name: _____
1.	
2.	
3.	
4.	

An Interview:

With another student, do an imaginary interview with one of the characters you have met so far in the novel. Together, create at least <u>six</u> interesting questions to ask your subject, and then put together possible answers to each of the questions. You may also wish to enact the interview in front of the class.

1. _____

2. _____

3. _____

4. _____

5. _____

6. _____

ROLL OF THUNDER, HEAR MY CRY

BY MILDRED D. TAYLOR

Chapter 8

Before you read the chapter:

Cassie plans on getting revenge on Lillian Jean in this chapter. Why might this be very dangerous?

_____

_____

_____

_____

Vocabulary:

Choose a word from the list to complete each definition.

sentinel	saunter	irritable	morose	securely	ventured
feigned	destruction	reassurance	jovial	passionate	resentful

1. The convict _____ indifference when asked if he was sorry for his behavior.

2. The _____ of the chicken coop by the tornado was more than my grandmother could bear.

3. He stood by the compound gate like a _____ for the entire weekend.

4. No one _____ outside during the hurricane.

5. Uncle Festus was in a most _____ mood during the party.

6. Tim is very _____ about stamp-collecting.

7. It was very annoying to watch him _____ casually by, knowing that he was guilty.

8. When teething, babies are usually very _____.

© On The Mark Press • S&S Learning Materials   39   OTM-14276 • SSN1-276 Roll of Thunder, Hear My Cry

ROLL OF THUNDER, HEAR MY CRY
BY MILDRED D. TAYLOR

9. Make sure that small children are _____ fastened in their car seats.

10. The players on the losing team needed their coach's _____ that they still had a chance next game.

11. Following the death of his pet turtle, I found my sister to be quite _____.

12. Parents who play favorites will often find their children increasingly _____ of their actions.

Questions:

1. a) Describe briefly how Cassie taught Lillian Jean a lesson without getting herself into trouble.

    _____

    _____

    _____

    _____

    _____

    b) What did Cassie mean by the statement: "Lillian Jean didn't even realize it had all been a game?"

    _____

    _____

2. What does the following expression mean (you may need to check the context of the quote): "I got too many worries of my own to worry 'bout Cassie Uncle Tomming Lillian Jean?"

    _____

    _____

3. Think of an example of what Papa was speaking of in the following quote: "Cassie, there'll be a whole lot of things you ain't gonna wanna do but you'll have to do in this life just so you can survive."

_____

_____

4. Papa tells Cassie that the way to gain respect is: "How you carry yourself, what you stand for – that's how you gain respect." How else is it possible to gain the respect of others?

_____

_____

5. Why did the three men come to sit in on Mama's lesson? What did they find objectionable? What was their real motive for what they did?

_____

_____

_____

_____

6. What offer did Mr. Morrison make to Papa?

_____

_____

7. How had T.J. been partially responsible for getting Mama fired?

_____

_____

_____

ROLL OF THUNDER, HEAR MY CRY
BY MILDRED D. TAYLOR

Extension Activities:

Roll of Thunder, Hear My Cry is a novel featuring a number of dramatic conflicts – some verbal, some physical (like the one between Cassie and Lillian Jean in Chapter 8). Choose one of the conflicts described thus far and complete the **Conflict Dissection Chart** below with as much detail as possible.

Characters Involved	**Setting** (Time, Place)
Problem (Details of the Conflict)	**Solution/Resolution**

ROLL OF THUNDER, HEAR MY CRY
BY MILDRED D. TAYLOR

Chapter 9

Before you read the chapter:

To this point in the novel, the plot has been building toward a great crisis. In order for a crisis to develop effectively, a novel usually requires characters known as **antagonists**. (The good guys are called **protagonists**.) It is especially essential that the antagonists are portrayed as being really dangerous. <u>Who</u> do you consider to be the antagonists of this novel, and why are they so menacing?

_____

_____

_____

_____

Vocabulary:

Synonyms are words with similar meanings. Using the context of the sentences below, choose the best synonym for the underlined words in each sentence.

1. Cousin Jeffrey's voice was **<u>audible</u>** from his bedroom.
   a) muffled   b) discernible   c) mentioned   d) impulsive

2. The cherry tree seemed to **<u>droop</u>** in the heat of the summer day.
   a) disappear   b) whisper   c) hide   d) sag

3. My uncle **<u>resigned</u>** his position at the car factory.
   a) quit   b) gained   c) sheltered   d) protected

4. Papa was very **<u>exasperated</u>** at the antics of his children.
   a) pleased   b) frustrated   c) amused   d) fatigued

5. All her classmates agreed that Lillian Jean was a very **<u>persnickety</u>** girl.
   a) vengeful   b) excitable   c) fussy   d) joyous

ROLL OF THUNDER, HEAR MY CRY
BY MILDRED D. TAYLOR

6. "Will you please **summon** the other children to dinner," Mama said.
   a) call   b) bully   c) escort   d) email

7. Their mansion had many **amenities** that most people can only dream of.
   a) swimming pools   b) furniture   c) rooms   d) comforts

8. Do you think that Sally Jean will **venture** another guess after her humiliation?
   a) hesitate   b) risk   c) take back   d) hazard

9. His offer to help Papa on that morning was a bit **premature**.
   a) simple   b) bold   c) early   d) awkward

10. It is not a good idea to **rile** Sheriff Coffey.
    a) anger   b) interrupt   c) doubt   d) strike

Questions:

1. Why do you think R.W. and Melvin let T.J. hang out with them?

   _____

   _____

2. Do you agree with Mama that T.J. *just wants attention*? Please explain your answer.

   _____

   _____

3. What did Mr. Jamison come to warn the Logans about?

   _____

   _____

4. How did Mr. Granger put the squeeze on the other families in the area?

   _____

   _____

5. Why was it necessary financially for Papa to work on the railway when they had such a large piece of land to farm?

   _____

   _____

ROLL OF THUNDER, HEAR MY CRY
BY MILDRED D. TAYLOR

6. Papa compares life to a fig tree. Other than a tree or plant, what else might he have used as an illustration? Why?

_____

_____

7. Find a possible example of foreshadowing in this chapter. (Hint: It has to do with T.J.)

_____

_____

8. Write a brief synopsis of what happened to Papa and the others on their trip to Vicksburg.

_____

_____

_____

_____

_____

Language Activities:

1. Copy out any three sentences from this chapter and underline the verbs.

_____

_____

_____

_____

_____

2. Beside each of the following words from the novel, write its **root word**.

a) producing _____   e) premature _____

b) gently _____   f) planned _____

c) distastefully _____   g) sharply _____

d) unforgiving _____   h) running _____

3. The word "**slave**" can be used as a **noun** or a **verb**, depending on the sentence. Use your imagination and write sentences to illustrate how this word can be used as both a noun and a verb.

a) **Slave as a Noun:** _____

_____

b) **Slave as a Verb:** _____

_____

Extension Activity:

Observation Chart

How careful an observer are you? *Roll of Thunder, Hear My Call* is a novel rich with sights, sounds, and smells. Review the chapters you have read thus far and collect as many examples of the five senses as you can find. These examples should be listed in the chart below. An example of **sound** is found in Chapter 9: "Mr. Avery's coughing started again and for a while there was only the coughing and the silence." See if you can get at least one example for each sense.

SIGHT: _____
_____

SOUND: _____
_____

TOUCH: _____
_____

TASTE: _____
_____

SMELL: _____
_____

ROLL OF THUNDER, HEAR MY CRY
BY MILDRED D. TAYLOR

Chapter 10

Before you read the chapter:

In this chapter, the Logan family have to make some serious sacrifices to keep their land. Tell about a time when you (or a friend) saved your money to buy something you really wanted.

_____

_____

_____

_____

Vocabulary:

Synonyms are words with similar meanings. Draw a line from each word in column A to its synonym in column B. Then use the words in column A to fill in the blanks in the sentences below.

Column A	Column B
1. hesitate	a) lazy
2. caution	b) endure
3. despondent	c) pause
4. phenomenal	d) interrupt
5. desolate	e) sad
6. lethargic	f) clear
7. condescending	g) determned
8. persist	h) sensational
9. disrupt	i) lonely
10. adamant	j) careful
11. distinct	k) patronizing

ROLL OF THUNDER, HEAR MY CRY
BY MILDRED D. TAYLOR

1. "Don't be so _____ to your mother," she said. "Treat people as you would have them treat you."

2. "I'm afraid I am going to have to be most _____ in directing you to the right doctor," my aunt said.

3. His voice was not as _____ as it might have been because of the noise of the crowd.

4. I'm not sure if you realize how _____ the island is.

5. The crowd's unpleasant reaction caused him to _____ for a few seconds.

6. Following the death of his parrot, the pirate was _____ for several days.

7. The convict's lawyer will be sure to _____ him about keeping curfew.

8. If you _____ in forgetting to take out the garbage, it will soon attract raccoons.

9. The hot weather made everyone feel quite disinterested and _____.

10. The heckler began to _____ the meeting with his constant catcalls.

11. Their all-star right winger has a _____ slap shot.

Questions:

Indicate whether the following statements are **True** or **False**.

1. Mama suggested they borrow money from Mr. Granger to pay the mortgage.   T   or   F

2. Mr. Morrison went looking for work.   T   or   F

3. Mr. Morrison lifted Kaleb Wallace's truck off the road.   T   or   F

4. Mr. Morrison said that Kaleb Wallace needed two things before taking a stand: lots of folks to back him up and a gun.   T   or   F

5. Jeremy suggested that T.J. had stolen Moe Turner's father's pistol.   T   or   F

6. The Logans didn't go to the sheriff after Papa was hurt because they were afraid Mr. Morrison would go to jail.   T   or   F

7. Jeremy told them that he had moved his bedroom to the loft in the barn.   T   or   F

8. The bank informed the Logan family that their credit was no good anymore. **T** or **F**

9. Uncle Hammer sold his home in Chicago to raise money to pay the mortgage. **T** or **F**

10. T.J. and the Wallace boys were planning on going into town to get the pearl-handled pistol. **T** or **F**

Language Activity:

Find three examples of the following parts of speech from this chapter.

Nouns	Verbs	Adjectives
_____	_____	_____
_____	_____	_____
_____	_____	_____

Extension Activity:

Interview at least three other students for their views of this novel thus far. (Try to get both positive and negative comments.)

Write a brief **report** putting these views together.

_____

_____

_____

_____

_____

_____

ROLL OF THUNDER, HEAR MY CRY

BY MILDRED D. TAYLOR

Extension Activities:

We have already read about a number of important conflicts in this novel.

Conflict is an important element in a novel. There are generally three types of conflict: **person against person; person against self;** and **person against nature.**

Find three examples of conflict in *Roll of Thunder, Hear My Cry* and tell which type of conflict each is. (You <u>don't</u> have to get an example from each category.)

1. _____

_____

_____

2. _____

_____

_____

3. _____

_____

_____

Write a **synopsis** of the events of Chapter 10.

_____

_____

_____

_____

_____

_____

_____

_____

_____

ROLL OF THUNDER, HEAR MY CRY
BY MILDRED D. TAYLOR

Chapter 11

Before you read the chapter:

Chapter Ten ends as a real *cliffhanger*. T.J. seems to be really torn between either following the Wallace boys into town to get the pearl-handled pistol **or** doing what he knows to be right. Predict what you think will happen next to T.J.

_____

_____

_____

_____

Vocabulary:

Analogies are equations in which the first pair of words has the same relationship as the second pair of words. For example, **stop** is to **go** as **fast** is to **slow**. In this example, both pairs of words are opposites. Choose the best word from the word box to complete each of the analogies below.

emerge	intended	frantic	despicable	sympathy	hoarse
nauseous	finality	ferocious	recite	vulnerable	eventual

1. **Later** is to _____ as **porch** is to **veranda**.

2. **Repeat** is to _____ as **black** is to **ebony**.

3. **Gentle** is to _____ as **older** is to **younger**.

4. **Harmony** is to _____ as **pale** is to **ashen**.

5. **Decisiveness** is to _____ as **spouse** is to **mate**.

6. **Disappear** is to _____ as **night** is to **day**.

7. **Worry** is to **fret** as **meant** is to _____.

ROLL OF THUNDER, HEAR MY CRY

BY MILDRED D. TAYLOR

8. **Behind** is to **ahead** as **lovable** is to _____.

9. **Courageous** is to **cowardly** as **calm** is to _____.

10. **Value** is to **cherish** as **susceptible** is to _____.

11. **Healthy** is to _____ as **valuable** is to **worthless**.

12. **Gruff** is to _____ as **cure** is to **remedy**.

Questions:

1. Why do you think the author begins this chapter with a poem?

   _____

   _____

2. Describe the circumstances leading to T.J.'s late-night visit to the Logans' house.

   _____

   _____

   _____

   _____

3. Why did Mrs. Barnett assume the two Wallace boys were black?

   _____

   _____

4. When the children arrived at T.J.'s house, what complicated the situation?

   _____

   _____

5. When the Logan children were watching the mob attack T.J. and his family, what do you think Cassie meant when she said, "I watched the world from outside myself?"

_____

_____

6. Who arrived at the Averys' place to try to protect T.J.?

_____

_____

7. When Stacey told Cassie to return home to get Papa, why was she afraid to leave her older brother?

_____

_____

Extension Activities:

Collage

Make a collage from magazine pictures illustrating a scene from the novel, or events and characters from the entire novel.

Talk Show

With two or three other students prepare to participate in a television talk show featuring characters from this novel. Choose a couple of interesting characters from the book (possibly one of the Logans and someone like T.J. or one of the Wallaces). Prepare about a half-dozen questions to ask and possible answers.

ROLL OF THUNDER, HEAR MY CRY
BY MILDRED D. TAYLOR

Chapter 12

Before you read the chapter:

Before you begin reading the novel's final chapter, would you read <u>another</u> novel by the author, Mildred D. Taylor? Why or why not?

_____

_____

_____

_____

Vocabulary:

Choose a word from the list to complete each definition:

adamant	trench	transfixed	stricken	singe
intend	remnant	menacing	clenched	billow

1. Someone who is deeply affected is _____.

2. If someone plans to do something, they _____ to do it.

3. A person whose actions or words are considered threatening is _____.

4. To _____ is to swell out or bulge.

5. To stop what you are doing and stare wordlessly at something is to be _____.

6. A _____ is a deep ditch.

7. To burn slightly is to _____.

8. Someone who is _____ is a very convicted person.

9. Something held tightly in one's hand is _____.

10. Something left over is a _____.

ROLL OF THUNDER, HEAR MY CRY
BY MILDRED D. TAYLOR

Questions:

1. How did Cassie's parents discover that the children were missing in the middle of the night?

   _____

   _____

2. What did Mama try to convince Papa not to take with him when he went to the Averys'?

   _____

   _____

3. According to Mama, how did the fire start?

   _____

   _____

4. Why did they have to stop the fire before it reached the trees?

   _____

   _____

5. The climax of a story occurs when the main problem of the story is solved. When does the climax of this novel occur?

   _____

   _____

6. Describe how the lynching party was distracted from their original purpose.

   _____

   _____

ROLL OF THUNDER, HEAR MY CRY
BY MILDRED D. TAYLOR

7. What was the reason Mr. Jamison gave to Papa for staying clear of this whole thing?

_____

_____

8. How did Mr. Jamison think the fire had started?

_____

_____

9. Describe your feelings about this novel. What was one thing you really enjoyed, and something you think that the author might have improved?

_____

_____

Language Activities:

Antonyms, Synonyms or Homonyms

Beside each pair of words write **A** (antonym) or **S** (synonym) or **H** (homonym).

1. die – dye _____

2. little – enormous _____

3. red – read _____

4. cry – sob _____

5. pasture – grass _____

6. here – hear _____

7. tight – loose _____

8. way – weigh _____

9. kill – slay _____

10. do – dew _____

ROLL OF THUNDER, HEAR MY CRY
BY MILDRED D. TAYLOR

Storyboard

A storyboard is a series of pictures that tell the main events of a story. A storyboard can tell the story of only one scene – or the entire novel.

Complete the storyboard below illustrating your favorite scene from Roll of Thunder, Hear My Cry. You may wish to practice your drawings on a separate piece of paper

1	2
3	4
5	6

ROLL OF THUNDER, HEAR MY CRY

BY MILDRED D. TAYLOR

Extension Activity:

Create a **book cover** for <u>Roll of Thunder, Hear My Cry</u>. Be sure to include the title, author, and a picture that will make other students want to read the novel.

ROLL OF THUNDER, HEAR MY CRY
BY MILDRED D. TAYLOR

Lights, Camera, Action!

Roll of Thunder, Hear My Cry was made into a movie in 1978 and was nominated for two Primetime Emmy Awards. The movie was shot in the form of a three part miniseries for television and starred Lark Ruffin as Cassie and Claudia McNeil as Big Ma. The well-known actor, Morgan Freeman, played the role of Uncle Hammer.

Complete either Part A or B.

Part A

Find a copy of the video, **Roll of Thunder, Hear My Cry**, and after viewing the film, write a review. This review can be posted on a website such as **www.amazon.com.**
Your review should contain a brief synopsis of the movie (without giving away the ending), and state your impression of the movie (positive and negative). You may also wish to compare the movie with the novel – what was the same and what changes were made by the producers.
Your review should be at least a half-page in length.

Part B

You are the casting director for a project designed to put together an updated version of **Roll of Thunder, Hear My Cry.** Who would you cast for the principal roles?:

Cassie: _____

Stacey: _____

T.J.: _____

Big Ma: _____

Mama: _____

Papa: _____

Uncle Hammer: _____

Little Man: _____

Mr. Morrison: _____

You may wish to choose Hollywood actors for this task, or for a bit of fun, limit your choices to people in your school (teachers and students). Beside each choice, write a brief explanation for your choice.

Answer Key

Chapter 1 *(page 10)*

Vocabulary:

1. meticulous   **2.** dubious   **3.** concession   **4.** admonish   **5.** restrain   **6.** amiable   **7.** disdain
8. morose   **9.** torment   **10.** imperious   **11.** vigorous   **12.** indignation

Questions:

1. To pay the mortgage and taxes on the land
2. *Answers will vary.* (i.e., He sacrificed to buy land to benefit future generations of the family.)
3. T.J. said Claude had snuck up to the store to get free candy and he only went there to bring him back.
4. By a passing school bus
5. The teacher of the grade one class, Miss Davis, had been held up in Jackson for a few days.
6. **a)** The word "nigra" was written inside the front cover.
   b) *Answers will vary.*
7. *Answers will vary.* (i.e., She has probably gotten used to the way black people are treated and is just grateful to get the books for their school.)
8. *Answers will vary.*
9. 1. (b)   2. (d)   3. (a)   4. (e)   5. (f)   6. (c)

Chapter 2 *(page 14)*

Vocabulary:

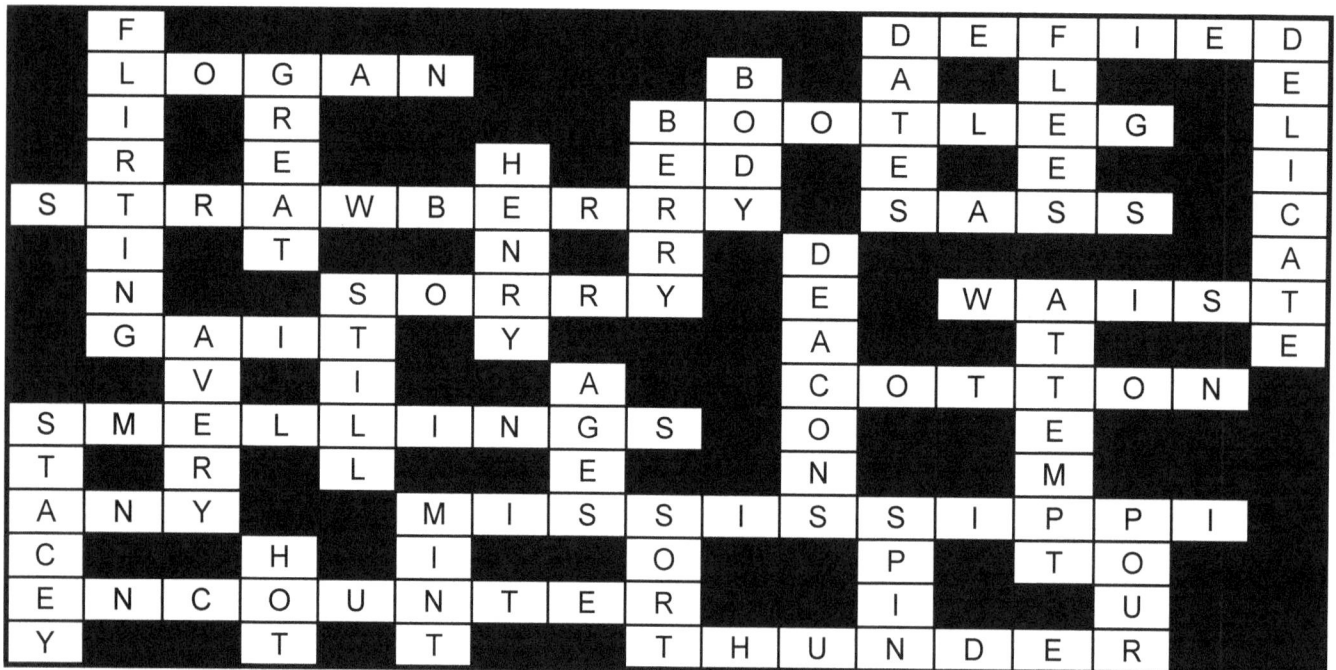

Questions:

1. a) He was enormous - tall and muscular. Looked like his face and neck had been scarred by fire.
   b) He had lost his job on the railroad and couldn't find work.
   c) To protect the family when Papa was away.
2. He was black, the other men were white.
3. The Wallaces sold bootleg liquor and cigarettes to children.
4. *Answers will vary.*
5. He was going to take a switch to their bottoms.

Extension Activities:
a) seeds   b) King   c) bolls   d) thread

Chapter 3 *(page 18)*

Vocabulary:

1. unmovable	**2.** resentful	**3.** lonely	**4.** realize	**5.** command
6. reckless	**7.** delicious	**8.** approve	**9.** laughable	**10.** startle

Questions:

By the end of <u>October</u>, the rain began to fall heavily. To shield the children against the rain, Mama gave them dried <u>calfskins</u>. To keep dry, however, the children preferred the shelter of the overhanging <u>limbs</u> in the forest. Mama explained to Little Man that money which supported the black schools came from the black <u>churches</u>. After being splashed by the passing bus one particular day, <u>Stacey</u> promised Little Man that it wouldn't happen again, at least not for a long while. At <u>lunch</u> hour, the children took some shovels from the <u>tool</u> shed and dug a hole in the middle of the road. The hole quickly filled with <u>water</u>. That evening on the way home, the children watched as the <u>bus</u> got stuck in the hole. Mr. <u>Grimes</u>, the driver, was extremely upset. At home that evening, the children were surprised when <u>Mama</u> said she was glad the bus had gotten stuck. Later that evening, Joe <u>Avery</u> came by to warn them that the night men were riding. Little Man was afraid that the night men were going to come and <u>burn</u> them up. Later, when Cassie went outside, she was frightened by <u>Jason</u>, their hound dog. Just when she was about to go back to bed, a caravan of <u>headlights</u> appeared in the east, coming toward her. After the cars left, Cassie could see Mr. <u>Morrison</u> standing in the darkness, a <u>shotgun</u> in his hand.

Chapter 4 *(page 22)*

Vocabulary:
1. (k)   **2.** (h)   **3.** (a)   **4.** (j)   **5.** (b)   **6.** (i)   **7.** (c)   **8.** (d)   **9.** (l)   **10.** (g)   **11.** (e)   **12.** (f)

Questions:
1. By stirring; milk cream fat globules come together clumping into lumps of butter, leaving a liquid called butter milk.
2. She isn't eating properly; she isn't sleeping right; she won't go out and play.
3. They acted disinterested.
4. Mr. Tatum called Jim Lee Barnett a liar. They tarred and feathered him.
5. *Answers will vary.* (i.e., He liked his privacy and the solitude.)
6. *Answers will vary.* (i.e., With Papa gone, Stacey, as the oldest male, felt Mr. Morrison was taking Papa's place instead of him).
7. a) *Answers will vary.*
   b) Stacey wanted to fight T.J., but T.J. ran into the store.
8. He told Stacey and the others that he expected them to tell their Mama about the incident. *Answers will vary.* (i.e., he was wise, understanding.)
9. *Answers will vary.* (i.e., He was greedy and obsessed with the past when his family owned that piece of land.)
10. The Wallaces poured kerosene on him and set him on fire.
11. She stopped at a number of their neighbors and urged them to keep their children from going there.

Language Activities:

1. children **2.** men **3.** buses **4.** buddies **5.** classes
6. gullies **7.** folks **8.** families **9.** matches **10.** berries

Chapter 5 *(page 27)*

Vocabulary: **1.** prevail **2.** denied **3.** obvious **4.** obnoxious **5.** Envision **6.** ambled
7. warily **8.** reluctant **9.** persisted **10.** moderate **11.** disgust **12.** retaliate

Questions:

1. T.J. was coming and Big Ma found him to be obnoxious, so she wanted T.J. kept occupied.
2. 3:30 A.M.
3. Disappointment
4. The white folks had their booths there.
5. *Answers will vary.*
6. *Answers will vary.*

Language Activities:

Alphabetical Order: sense, several, shingles, Stacey, Strawberry, subdued, such, suggestion, suppose, surprisingly

Chapter 6 *(page 30)*
Vocabulary:

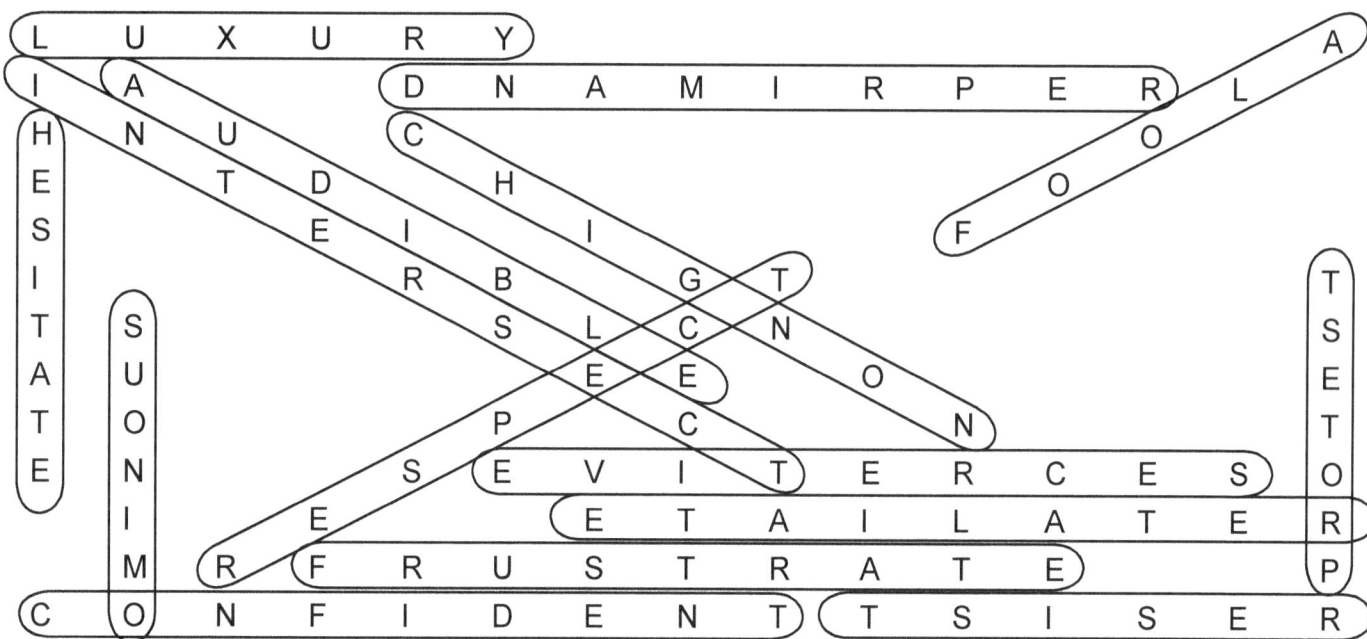

Questions:

1. *Answers will vary.* (i.e., She didn't want Cassie to get into further trouble with Simms.)
2. Hammer would have done something rash and got killed. She could have cautioned Cassie beforehand about saying anything about the incident to Hammer.
3. *Answers will vary.* (i.e., The black people were subject to the cruelty of many whites in that society.)
4. *Answers will vary.*
5. He had a knowledge of herbs and cures.
6. *Answers will vary.* (i.e., She learned how cruel and dangerous other people can be and how vulnerable she and her family were.)
7. He went for a ride with him to give him time to cool off and talked some sense into him.
8. *Answers will vary.* (i.e., jealousy).

Language Activities
1. Cassie and Stacey drove into Strawberry in Uncle Hammer's Packard.
2. Why don't you go to Boston for the Christmas holiday?
3. France, Germany, and Belgium are all European countries.

Chapter 7 *(page 34)*
Vocabulary: *Answers will vary.*

Questions:
1. *Answers will vary.*
   b) He was sorry for the way he acted with T.J.
2. She knew he wouldn't fly off the handle like Hammer and do something rash.
3. Certain slaves were chosen for their strength to have children together.
4. Dumas' father was a mulatto and his grandma was a slave.
5. *Answers will vary.* (i.e., They were poor and probably wouldn't be having much of a Christmas.)
6. *Answers will vary.*
7. *Answers will vary.* (i.e., Although he treasured the gift, he didn't think it was appropriate to display these feelings to his Papa).
8. In case she died, there wouldn't be any complications passing the land to her family.
9. To back the credit of the local families wishing to shop in Vicksburg.
10. He threatened to raise the rent on his lands for the sharecroppers.
11. *Answers will vary.* (i.e., They can all be killed.)

Chapter 8 *(page 39)*
Vocabulary: 1. feigned   **2.** destruction   **3.** sentinel   **4.** ventured   **5.** jovial   **6.** passionate
7. saunter   **8.** irritable   **9.** securely   **10.** reassurance   **11.** morose   **12.** resentful

Questions:
1. a) She became her friend, learned all her secrets, then beat her up (without leaving any marks) and threatened to tell everyone her secrets if she told anyone what happened.
   b) Answers will vary. (i.e., She didn't understand Cassie's point of view.)
2. An African-American is considered an "Uncle Tom" if he/she tries to ingratiate him/herself with white people at the expense of his/her self respect.
3. Answers will vary. (i.e., She will on occasion have to swallow her pride to make her life and lives of her loved ones less difficult.)
4. Answers will vary.
5. They sat in on her lesson because they had heard she was teaching "subversive" things about slavery. They found that she wasn't teaching from the approved textbook. They came to fire her.
6. To find a job to help with the expenses of the household.
7. He had told everyone at the store that Mrs. Logan had failed him on purpose. She had stopped everyone from coming to the store; She had destroyed school property.

Chapter 9 *(page 43)*
Vocabulary: 1. (b)   **2.** (d)   **3.** (a)   **4.** (b)   **5.** (c)   **6.** (a)   **7.** (d)   **8.** (b)   **9.** (c)   **10.** (a)

Questions:
1. *Answers will vary.* (i.e., They were taking advantage of him.)
2. *Answers will vary.*
3. Thurston Wallace was threatening to put a stop to the shopping in Vicksburg.
4. The sharecroppers would have to give him 60% of the cotton instead of usual 50%.

5. They didn't make enough from selling the cotton to pay the mortgage and taxes on the land.
6. *Answers will vary.* (i.e., a river or stream).
7. Mama says, "they'd better figure out some way of getting that boy back on the right track because he's headed for a whole lot of trouble."
8. *Answers will vary.* (They were stopped by three white men. Papa was shot and his leg was accidentally run over by the wagon. Mr. Morrison hurt a couple of their attackers and they left.)

Language Activities:
2. a) produce b) gentle c) taste d) forgive e) mature f) plan g) sharp h) run

Chapter 10 *(page 47)*
Vocabulary: 1. hesitate – pause **2.** caution – careful **3.** despondent – sad **4.** phenomenal - sensational; **5.** desolate – lonely **6.** lethargic – lazy **7.** condescending – patronizing **8.** persist – endure **9.** disrupt – interrupt **10.** adamant – determined **11.** distinct – clear.
1. condescending **2.** adamant **3.** distinct **4.** desolate **5.** hesitate **6.** despondent **7.** caution **8.** persist **9.** lethargic **10.** disrupt **11.** phenomenal

Questions: 1. False **2.** True **3.** True **4.** True **5.** False **6.** True **7.** False **8.** True **9.** False **10.** True

Chapter 11 *(page 51)*
Vocabulary: 1. eventual **2.** recite **3.** ferocious **4.** sympathy **5.** finality **6.** emerge **7.** intended **8.** despicable **9.** frantic **10.** vulnerable **11.** nauseous **12.** hoarse

Questions:
1. *Answers will vary.*
2. T.J. had been involved in the robbery of the mercantile in Strawberry with the Wallace boys. The owner and his wife had been injured, a pistol and other items were stolen. T.J. had been beaten up after the robbery by the Wallaces.
3. T.J. wasn't wearing a mask, and the Wallace boys were.
4. A group of townsmen arrived in their cars looking for T.J.
5. *Answers will vary.*
6. Mr. Jamison
7. She was afraid he would try to help T.J. and be hurt or killed.

Chapter 12 *(page 54)*
Vocabulary: 1. stricken **2.** intend **3.** menacing **4.** billow **5.** transfixed **6.** trench **7.** singe **8.** adamant **9.** clenched **10.** remnant

Questions:
1. Mr. Morrison happened to go by and see the door open.
2. The shotgun.
3. Lightning.
4. It would destroy everything all the way to Strawberry.
5. Answers will vary. (i.e., When the fire is brought under control.)
6. They left the lynching to fight the fire.
7. He advised David to lay low and let people think that he was a victim of the fire.
8. Mr. Logan set it.
9. Answers will vary.

Language Activities: 1. H **2.** A **3.** H **4.** S **5.** S **6.** H **7.** A **8.** H **9.** S **10.** H

www.ingramcontent.com/pod-product-compliance
Lightning Source LLC
Chambersburg PA
CBHW080523090426

42734CB00015B/3145